KNOW Your HORSES

Jack Byard

Old Pond Publishing

First published 2009, reprinted 2009,2010

ISBN 978-1-906853-01-3

Published by:
Old Pond Publishing Ltd
Dencora Business Centre
36 White House Road
Ipswich IP1 5LT
United Kingdom

www.oldpond.com

Old Pond Publishing are proud to support the Suffolk Punch Trust.

Book design by Liz Whatling
Printed and bound in China

Contents

Measurements are given in 'hh' meaning 'hands high'. For more information see 'Horse Talk' at the end of the book.

Acknowledgements

It is hard to believe it is a year since my first *Know Your...* book was published,
and now here we are with number four.

These words and images would not leave my ageing grey cells or my computer were it not
for the unstinting help given by all the Associations and Societies, large and small, who
never seem to tire of my endless questions and queries, at least, not to my face.

A special thank you to the team at Old Pond Publishing without whose faith and energy
I would be having a quiet retirement.

Picture Credits

Plate *(1)* Emily Oakes and Louise Parker, *(2)* Sand Creek Stud, Devon, *(3)* Alemany Bird, *(4)* Mannog Appaloosas, *(5)* Jenny Lees, *(6)* Droit Réserve Haras Nationaux, *(7)* Heidi Colling – Spanish Barb Breeders Association, *(8)* HeavyHorse Hills – Custom horse drawn carriage service (Zeus), *(9)* Rebecca Moore, *(10)* Chanfouti C. French National Studs 'Nenuphar', Boulonnais draught horse national stallion, *(11)* Brenda Duncan, *(12)* Zoe and Alan, Swordale Knockandu Stud, *(13)* Condomines J.-L/HN, *(14)* British Connemara Pony Society, *(15)* Sussex Polo - 'Carlita', *(16)* Gill Bridgeman, *(17)* www.whintordartmoors.com, *(18)* Black Forest and Gypsy Horses, *(19)* Ron Le Poole, *(20)* Zamora, owned by Richard Chong – Dutch Equine Stables, *(21)* Donald McGillivray, *(22)* Jane Lillis, *(23)* Helen Underwood-Thomas, *(24)* Brackenbank Fell Ponies, *(25)* Fjord-Crown Jewel Resort Ranch, *(26)* Friesians4all, *(27)* Oakbriar Hackneys, *(28)* Deer Haven Farm, Lexington, Kentucky, USA, *(29)* Mrs Alison Mcleod, *(30)* Quainton Stud, *(31)* Jill Noble, Pentland Hills Icelandics, Carlops, *(32)* The Irish Cob Society, *(33)* Norma Grubb, *(34)* Sine Møller, *(35)* Aurelio Grilopen Llyn Luisitanos, *(36)* Aga Jasko, *(37)* Martin O'Neil, *(38)* Linda Chapman, *(39)* Kerswell Stud, *(40)* The Shire Horse Society, *(41)* Bunting and Sons, *(42)* 'Coax Kid' standing at stud in NY, USA. Owned by Troy M.Wing/Sunnydale Stables, *(43)* Dr Wynne Davies MBE, *(Ponies Needing Protection)* Kaimanawa Wild Horse Welfare Trust; Jane Mullen; Zoe Lucas, Sable Island Green Horse Society.

Foreword

I am of an age to have experienced many things in life. I have seen and heard many beautiful things as well as much I would prefer to forget. Whilst writing these books I have never become accustomed to a feeling of sadness when I read about animals becoming extinct or verging on extinction.

I realise that breeders have a commercial interest in their animals and have a responsibility to their families and employees. The harsh reality of the commercial world is, 'If it doesn't make a profit I cannot keep it.' As a result, the fate of many rare and at-risk breeds lands firmly on the shoulders of smallholders and farmers who are able to keep the animals for pleasure as well as profit.

In Britain we have the Rare Breeds Survival Trust which protects at-risk species and there are similar societies throughout the world. If we let any one of these endangered breeds become extinct we are losing even more than the horses; we are losing part of our history and heritage. It is not easy when money is short and the credit crunch bites but extinction is not an option. The solution is in our hands.

JACK BYARD
Bradford, 2009

American Bashkir Curly

Native to
Origins unknown

Now found
Mainly in America but also in the British Isles, Europe, Canada and Australia

Size
14.2hh – 15.2hh

Description

The American Bashkir Curly comes in all horse colours.

There are many theories about the ancestors of the Amercian Bashkir Curly. The main contender was the Russian Bashkir (hence the name) but technology has proved beyond a doubt that they are not related. The mystery remains. The name has not been changed in order to avoid confusion in public recognition.

The Lakota Sioux and the Crow Native Americans used the Curly, which was considered sacred and owned only by tribal chiefs and medicine men. Native American drawings show the Curly at the Battle of the Little Big Horn. In the late 19th century Giovanni Demele, an Italian immigrant living in Nevada, saw the Curly and started to breed them.

The Curly is friendly, trusting and very quick to learn. The hair resembles mohair rather than horse hair and is hypoallergenic; people allergic to straight-haired horses seldom have a reaction to the Curly. The appearance of the coat has been described as crushed velvet and a wave. The manes and tails vary from ringlets to dreadlocks.

American Paint Horse

Native to
America

Now found
Worldwide

Size
14.2hh – 15.2hh

Description

Black, brown, bay, bay roan, blue roans, dun, grey, chestnut, palomino, red dun and red roan.

The Spanish explorer Hernando Cortes set sail for the New World in 1519 surrounded by an army of Conquistadors and a number of horses. The expedition's historian Diaz del Castillo recorded that one of the horses was a pinto with white socks and another was a dark roan with white patches.

In the early 19th century the American plains had a great number of feral horses. Some had unusually coloured patterned coats and, because their brilliant appearance matched their ability and performance, they soon became the horse of choice for the Native American Indian; particularly the Comanche.

At the beginning of the 20th century Paint Horse numbers declined along with the decline in the traditional Western way of life and the rise in motorised transport. It was left to a few individuals to save the breed and in 1962 the American Paint Horse Association came into being, dedicated to preserving the bloodline and colour of this intelligent agile horse.

3.

Andalusian

Native to
The area of the Iberian
Peninsula that is now Spain.

Now found
Worldwide

Size
15.2hh – 16.2hh

Description

Most are grey, but bay, black and chestnut also occur in purebreds.

The Andalusian, also called the Purebred Spanish Horse, is one of the oldest horse breeds in the world. Cave paintings in the Iberian Peninsula show horses of the Andalusian type and these, along with archaeological evidence, suggest that the breed is at least 25,000 years old. It is recorded that the breed arrived on the shores of the British Isles 100 years after the Norman Conquest.

The ancient Greeks and Romans used the Andalusian as cavalry horses because of their remarkable agility and they proved themselves in battle over many centuries. During the 14th to 17th centuries the Classical Riding Academies used the Andalusian because of its natural balance and agility in High School Dressage.

In the 1800s numbers declined but the Carthusian monks kept faith with the Andalusian and maintained the purity of the breed. This horse is strong, sensitive and intelligent and, when treated with the respect it deserves, learns quickly.

Appaloosa

Native to
America

Now found
Throughout the British Isles and on most continents

Size
14.1hh – 15.1hh

Description

The colourful spotted coats have six pattern variations including leopard, as in this picture.

An ancient breed which is noted for its spotted coat pattern and whose ancestors go back 8,000 years. The Conquistadors brought some horses to America and by the 1700s these had reached the Pacific North West. It was here that the Nez Perce American Indians took to selectively breeding what was to become the Appaloosa. Only the finest of the stock were allowed to breed; inferior specimens were sold or gelded.

During the Nez Perce War in 1877 the tribe was hounded by the US Cavalry and finally caught only 30 miles from the safety of Canada. The Nez Perce were deprived of their land and horses and as a result the Appaloosa was pushed to the edge of extinction. Claude Thompson of Oregon saved the breed and there are now over 60,000 registered Appaloosas in America.

Ideal for riding, show jumping, carriage driving, polo, dressage and much more; the list of uses for this adaptable, hardy, gentle animal goes on.

Arabian

Native to
Arabia

Now found
Worldwide

Size
14.1hh – 15.1hh

Description

The Arabian is grey, chestnut, black or roan.

The Arabian is one of the oldest and most beautiful breeds of horse. It was highly prized by the Bedouin as a war horse and is known to have been living amongst the desert tribes of the Arabian Peninsula since 1000 years BC. The Arab was bred in harsh conditions so is able to survive on poor quality forage. In severe conditions the nomads would share food and water with their animals and when conditions were extreme the horses shared the tent. Genghis Khan, Napoleon, Alexander the Great and George Washington were all proud owners of Arabs.

Over many centuries the Arabian has been selectively bred; choosing only those animals which were alert and gentle, with intelligence and high spirits. Their qualities were essential for a war horse since speed and endurance were necessities.

Most modern horses have, somewhere in their long histories, been improved by Arabian blood to add stamina, speed or endurance. The breed excels in most equine activities and sports and is also a gentle, intelligent companion.

Ardennes

Native to
France

Now found
Worldwide

Size
15hh – 16hh

Description

The Ardennes is bay, roan or chestnut.

Originating in the Ardennes region of France, the Ardennes has ancestors going back 50,000 years which makes it one of the oldest horse breeds. In turn, most modern working horses are genetically linked to this breed which is descended from the Medieval 'Great Horse'. Carrying a knight in full battle armour is no easy task, but the breed was known for the tireless ease with which it worked.

The Ardennes has been used by the royal armies of the 17th and 18th centuries, Napoleon in his Russian campaign and during both World Wars where this docile animal made a welcome companion.

The modern Ardennes is used in all types of agriculture since it is less destructive than its mechanical counterpart. It is powered by home-grown fuel and the natural by-products fertilise the earth. Strong, gentle and willing; what more could you ask from a working companion.

7.

Barb

Native to
The Barbary coast of
North Africa

Now found
Small numbers are
found worldwide

Size
14.2hh – 15.2hh

Description

The Barb would seem to be most horse colours and patterns.

The Barb is a desert-bred horse believed to have been developed in North Africa. There is debate as to whether the Barb and the Arab share the same ancestors and which, if either, came first.

The Barb has influenced horse breeding worldwide since the spread of Islam brought it to Europe in the 8th century. It has played a major role in the development of the Andalusian, the Lusitano and some breeds within the British Isles.

Richard II was a proud Barb owner and Henry VIII imported several Barbs which later played an important role in the development of the Thoroughbred.

The Conquistadors took the Barb to the New World where, over the centuries, it has been used to develop American horses. Strong, brave, agile, it gallops like a sprinter and has great stamina.

Belgian Draught/ Brabant

Native to
Belgium

Now found
Throughout Europe
and in America

Size
16.1hh – 17hh

Description

Chestnut, sorrel or roan with a flaxen mane and tail.

The Belgian Draught or Brabant is the heavier relative of the mountain-bred Ardennes.

The Belgian is a direct descendant of the medieval Great Horse. These big, black Flemish horses, frequently written about by the scribes, had the speed and strength to carry an armoured knight into battle and were used by Caesar on his trips to Northern Europe. It is from this genetic pool that the majority of modern-day draught horses have developed.

At the end of the 19th century heavy draught horses were needed all over Europe for farm and industrial use so the Belgian was exported to Italy, France, Germany and Russia. The Belgian Government had been energetic in improving and refining the breed with excellent results so it was the obvious choice.

Today, the Belgian is ideal for the small farm where ecological awareness is a growing factor and they are popular as show and trail riding horses. They are quiet, willing and gentle.

Black Forest

Native to
Germany

Now found
Throughout Europe
and America

Size
15hh – 16hh

Description

The Black Forest is dark chestnut with a flaxen mane and tail.

The Black Forest horse originated over 600 years ago from, strangely enough, the Black Forest in the Baden-Württemberg region of Germany. The breed association only began in the later part of the 19th century and created a state registered breeding system. The association insisted that the farmers used only the Belgian Draught as stallions to 'improve' the Black Forest. Fortunately, the local farmers had more sense so ignored the directive and continued as they had for hundreds of years. The breed association eventually decided the 'improvement' was a mistake and local expertise and common sense prevailed.

The Black Forest horse has been an endangered breed for the last 25 years with only 1000 in existence but numbers are slowly increasing. The old heavy breeds are very versatile and now they pull smart brewer's drays and elegant wedding carriages. They also make an ideal leisure horse and are increasingly used for riding, especially therapeutic riding for children. Beautiful, gentle, durable and strong; a jewel in the equine world.

Boulonnais

Native to
France

Now found
Worldwide

Size
15hh – 16hh

Description

Mainly grey but a few are chestnut or bay.

The Boulonnais (meaning 'White Marble Horse') is believed to be descended from the horses Julius Caesar brought to Pas-de-Calais before invading the British Isles.

During the Crusades, breeders concentrated on breeding horses which were strong enough to carry a knight in full battle armour but still fast and agile.

During the 17th century Spanish occupation of Flanders, Andalusian, Barb and Arabian horses were imported. These were crossed with the native mares and the Boulonnais began. In the 17th century the breed was used for transporting fish speedily from Boulogne to Paris; the 200 mile *Route du Poisson* was covered in under 18 hours.

Originally, the Boulonnais was darker grey, but fashions changed and in the 1800s white horses were desirable so the standard was set for a pale grey horse which would appear white.

Cleveland Bay

Native to
Cleveland in England

Now found
Worldwide

Size
16hh – 16.2hh

Protection category

The Cleveland Bay is exclusively bay.

This is one of the oldest horse breeds in the British Isles. Throughout the Middle Ages the monasteries of the North East were the main horse breeders since packhorses were needed to transport trade goods between the monasteries.

It is believed that the female line of today's Cleveland Bay is descended from Yorkshire Dales packhorses. These were bred with the Barb, a desert horse from the Barbary Coast of North Africa. By the end of the 1600s the basis of the Cleveland Bay was in place and its popularity spread countrywide.

Over the next 100 years the Cleveland Bay became healthier and heavier and was used in agriculture as a draught horse. Mechanisation saw the fall in numbers of this beautiful, intelligent and adaptable animal. A group of dedicated breeders saved the Cleveland Bay from extinction. A team of Cleveland Bays is kept at the Royal Mews and make ideal heavy hunters and police horses.

Clydesdale

Native to
Scotland

Now found
Worldwide

Size
17hh and over

Protection category

Description

Most common colour is bay. Brown with white markings, black, grey, roan and chestnut are less common. White on the face, feet and legs is characteristic.

The Clydesdale is 'The Pride of Scotland' and a native to the country. The breed originated in Clydesdale (now part of South Lanarkshire) in the 1700s. John Paterson of Lochlyloch imported a Flemish stallion from England which was crossed with the native Lanarkshire horses to improve their overall strength and ability. In 1808, a filly was bought which was descended from the original Flemish Stallion and all modern Clydesdales can be traced back to this mare. At the height of its popularity there were 140,000 Clydesdales working on Scottish farms.

World War II demanded increased food production and the increasing mechanisation saw numbers of working Clydesdales dwindle. The breed is now returning to use in logging, farming and, dressed in their finery, pulling bridal carriages. To see these beautiful, gentle, graceful animals at work and play is heart warming.

Comtois

Native to
The Franco-Swiss border

Now found
Throughout Europe

Size
14.3hh – 15.3hh

Description

Chestnut or bay with a flaxen mane and tail.

The Comtois was bred in the high Jura Mountains and the Franche-Comte region and has a history dating back to the 4th century AD. In the 16th century the Comtois was used to improve the breed from which it is thought to have descended, the Burgundy. It was also used by Louis XVI and Napoleon as both a cavalry horse and a draught horse for hauling heavy artillery. During the 19th century the breed was crossed with other draught horses, the Percheron and the Boulonnais.

In the early 1900s the Comtois was in danger of extinction and so was crossed with small Ardennes stallions to rebuild the population. This also created a much stronger animal. This cross was halted in 1925.

Being bred in a mountainous landscape has ensured that the breed is hardy and surefooted, which makes it the ideal animal to work the difficult hillside vineyards and haul timber in the pine forests of the Jura. The Comtois is a sound and willing riding horse with a gentle nature which is easy to train.

Connemara

Native to
The west coast of Ireland

Now found
Worldwide

Size
14.2hh

Description

Usually grey but can be bay, brown, dun, chestnut, black, roan, palomino or dark-eyed cream.

Remains of the Connemara pony's ancestors have been found in the peat bogs of Ireland. These remains are over 10,000 years old.

The strength, agility and hardiness of the Connemara are thanks to thousands of years surviving on the desolate moorland and rocky terrain of their wild natural environment. In the early years, local farmers would round up the wild ponies and tame them for work around the farm where they were used as pack animals to carry seaweed, potatoes, hay, peat and fertiliser in baskets strapped to their backs. They frequently worked in the harsh conditions on the west coast of Ireland. On Sunday they would be harnessed to a trap to take the family to and from church.

During the 1500s the merchants of Galway were importing Spanish Andalusian horses and it is believed that some Andalusian blood was introduced into the Connemara in an attempt to improve the breed. How can you improve this kind, intelligent and graceful animal?

Criollo

Native to
Argentina

Now found
On most continents

Size
13.2hh – 14.3hh

Description

The Criollo can be any horse colour which includes more than 100 known colour combinations.

The term 'Criollo' originally referred to animals and humans that were pure-bred Spanish and born in the Americas. In 1540 the Spaniards were forced to abandon Buenos Aires and up to 50 horses were released. Over the next 40 years the feral horse population reached 12,000. Being born in the wild, the Criollo has developed as a hardy, disease-resistant animal, with the ability to survive extremes of heat and cold or with little water in the dry grasses of the Pampas in South America.

During the 19th century the Criollo was interbred with several imported European breeds and its superb qualities were very nearly ruined.

In 1934 Dr Emilio Solanet took control of the Breeders Association and created the modern Criollo. It is now used as a cow horse by the Gauchos and is an ideal horse for pleasure riders. The Criollo, when crossed with a Thoroughbred, creates an excellent polo pony. The Criollo is trustworthy, fearless and independent.

16.

Dales

Native to
The Pennine hills
of Northern England

Now found
Throughout the British Isles,
Europe, Canada and the
USA

Size
14hh – 14.2hh

Protection category

Description

The Dales is normally black or brown, sometimes grey or bay and occasionally roan.

The Dales pony was used in the long-gone lead industry as a pack animal to haul lead and fuel. In this harsh environment and difficult terrain an animal requires an iron constitution and endurance. The pack load would be 2 cwt (102 kg) of lead and, carrying this weight, the pony would travel upwards of 200 miles a week.

Because of its all-round ability and strength the Dales Pony was a great favourite of the Yorkshire upland farmer. It was used by the army on many occasions as a pack animal and artillery pony but by the end of World War II the breed was on the point of extinction. A few dedicated breeders have worked hard for 50 years to pull the Dales Pony back from the brink and now 100 foals are registered each year.

The Dales is a first-class riding and driving pony and a good all-rounder. They are strong, agile, hardy, courageous, thrifty, calm and intelligent. They had to come from Yorkshire!

Dartmoor

Native to
The British Isles

Now found
On most continents, the Falklands and Namibia

Size
11.2hh – 12.2hh

Protection category
🐏 🐏 🐏

Description

Comes in bay, brown, black, grey, roan or chestnut.

Traces of domesticated ponies on Dartmoor go back 3500 years. Dartmoor is harsh, wild and exposed to all weathers. A place where only the strongest survive. This has been the home of the Dartmoor pony since the Middle Ages.

This hard-working animal was used in quarries to carry heavy loads of ore across the moors and by tin miners as pit ponies. When the mines closed some ponies found work on the local farms while others were turned loose on the moor to return to their wild state.

The purebred Dartmoor was in decline when in 1998 the Dartmoor Pony Moorland Scheme was established, in partnership with the Dartmoor Pony Society, to improve the bloodline of the ponies living on the commons of Dartmoor and ensure their suitability for the Dartmoor environment.

An ideal first pony, kind, gentle and willing, sturdy enough for family riding and competition driving. Please remember it is illegal to feed the ponies on Dartmoor.

Drum Horse

Native to
The British Isles

Now found
Worldwide

Size
16hh and over

Description

Piebald or skewbald.

The Drum Horse is named after the task they perform. In the book *All The Queen's Horses* it is defined as 'A coloured Shire horse trained for a specific and highly respected job.'

The Drum Horse is a large, strong, even-tempered animal used in Ceremonies of State in the British Isles. Throughout history many different types of horse have been used but strength is important for carrying two silver kettle drums and a rider since the weight exceeds 136kg. A quiet disposition is also essential. They must remain calm when surrounded by the people, noise and chaos of a parade ground. Not to mention the beat of the kettle drum reverberating in their ears.

At one time coloured Shire horses were a common sight, then a decision was taken that piebald and skewbald colours could no longer be registered as Shire horses. These 'rejects' were taken up by the Gypsies as draught horses and their qualities can be seen in the Gypsy (Irish) cob today. The breed captures the heart and imagination of all who see them. A truly beautiful horse.

Dutch Draught

Native to
Holland

Now found
Throughout Europe

Size
16hh on average

Description

Usually chestnut, bay or grey and occasionally black.

In 1918 the Brabant was crossed with the local Zeeland breed and the Belgian Ardennes to create the magnificent Dutch Draught. The Royal Society 'The Dutch Draft Horse' was created in 1914. The main purpose of breeding draught horses was to produce an animal that was large, solid and immensely strong. The traditional purpose of the Dutch Draught was for use in agriculture because ploughing heavy marine clay soil required great strength and endurance; a quality that many other breeds did not possess.

The Dutch Draught is the heaviest of the Dutch breeds and, despite its size, is gentle, quiet, intelligent and extremely nimble when needed. They also have a good, long working life.

Mechanisation has, as with many horse breeds, decimated numbers, although some good sound animals still exist. A gentle leviathan and a truly beautiful animal

Dutch Warmblood

Native to
The Netherlands

Now found
Worldwide

Size
15.2hh –16.2hh

Description

The Dutch Warmblood is the result of selectively breeding Dutch stock with English, French and German horses. The programme was initiated in the 1960s and the result is said by many to be the most successful breed to be developed in post-war Europe.

In the 1800s coaching and coach horses reached a peak. Horses from the British Isles including the Norfolk Trotter, the Yorkshire Coach Horse, the Cleveland and the Hackney were exported to Europe and crossed with local breeds. The resulting cross breed had to be able to pull a plough yet look elegant between the shafts of a carriage and whilst being ridden. This was the beginning of the modern sports horse. With the increase in mechanisation the breeding was directed to pleasure sports horses.

The Dutch Warmblood has over recent years had a remarkable rise to prominence in the international equestrian world. This superb modern horse is eager, reliable, intelligent and suitable for any discipline.

Eriskay

Native to
The Western Islands
of Scotland

Now found
Throughout the British Isles
and in France

Size
12hh – 13.2hh

Protection category

Description

Mainly grey with occasionally black or bay. Most foals are born black and turn grey with maturity. Sounds familiar.

The Eriskay pony is what remains of the native ponies which were found throughout the Scottish Western Islands until the middle of the 19th century. The ponies were well adapted to the meagre grazing and wet and windy conditions. Their dense waterproof coats protect them from the worst of the westerly gales.

The Western Isles ponies were used by crofters for carrying peat and seaweed in baskets, ploughing and family transport. The women and children looked after the crofts while the men were at sea and so temperament was important; only ponies that were hard working and comfortable around the crofters were used for breeding. On a number of the islands the ponies were 'improved' by crosses with the Norwegian Fjord and the Clydesdale. On Eriskay Island access was difficult so the breed remained pure. By 1970, due to mechanisation, only 20 ponies remained. A dedicated group came together to save this friendly, versatile animal.

Exmoor

Native to
The British Isles

Now found
Worldwide

Size
11.1hh – 12.3hh

Protection category

Description

Bay or any shade of brown with oatmeal coloured markings around the eyes.

It is believed that the Exmoor pony's ancestors migrated across the prehistoric land bridge from Alaska because fossilised remains found in Alaska show a remarkable resemblance to the Exmoor. Cross breeding has been minimal which means the Exmoor is the purest of British breeds. In the 16th century many thousands of these ponies roamed Exmoor.

In winter the Exmoor has a double coat. The outer coat is coarse and greasy giving waterproof protection while the under coat is fine soft hair. This coat is highly efficient: snow landing on the coat does not melt and has to be shaken off by the pony. At the base of the Exmoor's tail is a fan of short hair called a Snow Chute which channels away snow and water.

At the end of World War II only 50 ponies remained and for 40 years little was done to preserve this marvellous animal. There are now nearly 1200 but of this number only 450 are in a breeding situation. It is an ideal pony for riding, driving and jumping.

Falabella

Native to
Argentina

Now found
Worldwide

Size
8hh on average

Description

Bay, black, pintos and palominos.

Despite its diminutive size the Falabella is a perfectly proportioned horse and not a pony.

The development of the Falabella was started in 1868 by Patrick Newtell who used the Criollo as his base stock. On Patrick's death his son-in-law took over the breeding stock and introduced Welsh, Shetland and Thoroughbred blood to create the Falabella Miniature Horse. In the 1940s the Falabella Horse Breeders Association began.

In 1977 Lord and Lady Fisher of Kilverstone Wildlife Park in Norfolk bought four stallions and a number of mares from Señor Julio Falabella. Over the next 20 years they worked to raise the public profile of this beautiful horse in the British Isles and internationally. The Falabella is a rare breed with less than 1000 animals worldwide. They are intelligent and well-mannered with an excellent temperament and a character which shines through when trained.

Fell

Native to
Cumbria in England

Now found
Throughout the British Isles,
Europe and the USA

Size
13hh – 14hh

Protection category

Description

The Fell pony is a descendant of the wild European ponies which arrived on these shores 17,000 years ago. During the Roman occupation herds of Fell-type ponies roamed and grazed the area around Hadrian's Wall. When the Romans withdrew they left behind their war stallions which bred with these local ponies to produce the distinct regional characteristics of the Fell.

The Vikings used the Fell as a draught animal and in the 1400s they were used as pack animals to transport wool and local produce across the British Isles.

Since the times of the Roman invasion these ponies have hauled copper, lead, slate and iron ore. The coming of the railway had a dire effect on the Fell pony and it is now at risk.

Life on the northern fells is hard and grazing is poor so horses larger than the Fell pony would not find sufficient nutrition to survive the harsh environment. The Fell is strong and sure-footed which makes it ideal family transport since it is capable of carrying a heavy adult. Their gentle temperament makes the ponies ideal for young and inexperienced riders.

25.

Fjord

Native to
Norway

Now found
Throughout the British Isles and on most continents

Size
13.1hh – 14.3hh but always considered a horse

Description

The Fjord comes in varying shades of dun and beige, occasionally with a dark dorsal stripe running from poll to tail.

A most welcome Viking invader. The Fjord was the Viking war horse and pack animal; carvings of the breed have been found on Viking runestones. The Fjord's ancestors migrated to what is now Norway thousands of years ago.

The Fjord is a powerful and sure-footed animal which is capable of transporting a heavy burden on treacherous mountain paths. It is still used in remote regions of Norway and until quite recently was used as a pack horse by the Norwegian army. The Fjord is able to survive in harsh conditions where other horses would perish. This quality comes from a long history of pure breeding.

It is easy to teach and quick to learn, a calm, trusting, even-tempered animal. These abilities make it a perfect trekking horse. Its size and weight-bearing ability makes it an ideal horse for children and adults.

Friesian

Native to
The Netherlands

Now found
Worldwide

Size
15hh – 17hh

Description

Friesians are always black.

The Friesian has remained physically unchanged for centuries and its origins can be traced back to the medieval horses of the Crusaders. Apart from a period during the 80 year war (1568-1648) when there was crossbreeding with the Andalusian, the Friesian has remained pure.

In the British Isles 2000 years ago, Friesian troops, possibly mercenaries, were to be seen at Hadrian's Wall mounted on proud, elegant, black horses. William the Conqueror is also said to have used Friesian stallions at the Battle of Hastings in 1066.

Friesians were mainly used as draught animals so, farm mechanisation led to a reduction in numbers. Few owners could afford to keep them for the occasional ride or carriage work so by 1965 only 500 mares remained. Fortunately, a few obstinate breeders could afford to operate not-for-profit studs. The fortunes of the Friesian horse have changed and it is now used for carriage driving, dressage and as a show horse. They are beautiful, lively and reliable with a superb temperament.

27

Hackney

Native to
The British Isles

Now found
Worldwide

Size
14hh -16hh

Protection category

Description

The Hackney is bay, brown, chestnut and black.

The origins of the Hackney go back to the 14th century when the main roads were little more than cart tracks so a good riding horse with an excellent trot was the best and most comfortable option. The ancestors of the Hackney were highly regarded by the Tudor monarchy who passed laws regarding breeding and export to protect these beautiful animals.

In the early 1800s a flashy carriage drawn by an exquisite horse was a necessity for any Regency aristocrat. Horse-drawn vehicles became more sophisticated and a carriage of quality demanded a horse with a high stepping action. In the early 19th century the breed was improved with an infusion of Arab stallion blood which added refinement without undermining the qualities of the Hackney.

The Hackney is not an ideal riding horse but crossing it with a Thoroughbred produces an excellent jumping horse. The breed is calm, alert, spirited and beautiful.

28

Haflinger

Native to
Austria and Northern Italy

Now found
On most continents

Size
13.2hh – 15hh

Description

Rich golden brown to light gold, with a flaxen mane and tail.

The Haflinger was bred to work in the mountains of its home land, where it became acclimatised to harsh conditions and self-preservation, in agriculture, forestry and as a pack horse.

The ancestry of the Haflinger can be traced back to the Middle Ages; many theories exist as to the breed make up. These include, a cross between various European breeds and an Arab bloodline which dates to conflict in Central Europe in 55AD.

After World War I and the signing of the Treaty of San Germain, South Tyrol and Hafling became part of Italy and the breeding was reorganised in the Austrian Tyrol. In World War II Haflingers were used as draught and pack animals by the military.

The young Haflingers are raised in alpine pastures where the thin air develops their hearts and lungs. They do not start work until they are 4 years old but are frequently healthy and active at 40.

Though bred for mountain work they are equally at home in dressage, show jumping and therapeutic riding.

29

Highland

Native to
The Scottish Highlands
and Islands

Now found
Throughout the British Isles
and on most continents

Size
13.2hh – 14.2hh

Protection category

Description

Various shades of grey and dun with a characteristic dorsal stripe. They can also be brown, black or bay.

The Highland Pony is one of Scotland's oldest native breeds and carries the markings of an ancient equine family: a dorsal stripe; a shoulder stripe; and 'zebra' stripes on the legs.

They were originally used to work on Highland and Island crofts. Ploughing, hauling, forestry and transport were, and still are, the daily tasks of this strong, versatile and intelligent animal. The Highland also was used during the Boer War (1899 – 1902) and World War I. This strong, sure-footed animal is frequently used for trekking since it is able to carry riders of all ages.

A hardy animal capable of withstanding the harshest of weather, it has strong badger-like hair providing a waterproof overcoat and a soft dense undercoat. The pony can live out in all weathers. Its strength and kindly nature have made its popularity international. It would be difficult to find an equestrian event that does not include a Highland pony.

30

Holstein

Native to
Germany

Now found
On most continents

Size
16hh – 17hh

Description

The Holstein is bay, black, brown, chestnut or grey.

The Holstein originated in the Schleswig-Holstein marshlands of Germany during the 13th century. The area was famous in the Middle Ages for quality horses bred by the local monks until the Reformation when their property was handed to local landowners. These landowners realised the importance of the Holstein as war and work horses so continued to work on the breed. In 1686 laws were created to ensure the quality of the Holstein and incentives were offered to make it worthwhile.

Further improvements to the breed were carried out between the 16th and 18th centuries as the need for faster coach horses and lighter cavalry horses became apparent. The reputation of the Holstein grew throughout the 17th and 18th centuries and in 1797 the number of Holsteins exported reached 10,000.

In the mid 1940s Thoroughbred blood was introduced and created one of Germany's greatest horses. They are ideal for jumping, dressage and eventing and usually finish at the top in most international equine events.

31

Icelandic

Native to
Iceland

Now found
Throughout the British Isles,
Europe and the USA

Size
12hh – 14.2hh

Description

Any colour you can think of: bay; brown; chestnut; grey; skewbald; palomino and dun. The prize colour is silver dapple where the body is chocolate brown with a silver mane and tail.

The Icelandic is the horse of the Vikings. The horses were selected from Scandinavia, Britain and its islands and taken to Iceland in Viking longboats over a thousand years ago. They were used in agriculture and as transport through the deep ravines and rivers. The horses in Iceland are all descendants of this original Viking stock. According to a law passed in 982AD, no horse can be imported into Iceland and once one has left it can never return. The Icelandic is reputed to be the purest horse breed in the world.

The Icelandic is hardy with great strength and stamina, highly intelligent and extremely versatile. Apart from the usual gaits they have a four-beat running walk called Tölt and a Flying Pace which is used for racing. They have a luxurious main and tail and a very thick winter coat in great contrast to their sleek, fine, shiny summer coat.

32

Irish Cob

Native to
Ireland

Now found
Throughout the British Isles
and the USA

Size
14.1hh - 16.2hh

Description

Any horse colour, including roan, skewbald and piebald.

The Cob is one of Ireland's oldest recognised breeds and has been bred by the Irish traveller for many generations. Tracing the origins of the breed is not a simple task as it is a cross between the Clydesdale, Irish Draught, Dales, Connemara and Andalusian. In 1588, defeated at the Battle of Gravelines, the Spanish fleet attempted to return home through the North Atlantic but violent storms tore the fleet apart and 24 ships were wrecked on the north west coast of Ireland. Some of the Andalusians escaped and swam ashore. These survivors bred with the local horses.

For many hundreds of years the Cob was a hard working member of the Irish farming community and travellers criss-crossed the country in their barrel-topped wagons drawn by the Cob. The horses were members of the family so apart from being strong and hardy they had to be gentle and docile in nature. It is these qualities which make the Cob ideal as a family horse and for riding and driving.

33.

Irish Draught

Native to
Ireland

Now found
Worldwide

Size
15.1hh – 16.3hh

Description

The Irish Draught is bay, chestnut, black or grey.

The ancestors of the Irish Draught include the Irish Hobby horse and Spanish horses brought to Ireland during the Anglo-Norman invasion. Their development also included influences from the Connemara and Thoroughbred.

The Irish Draught has traditionally been bred as a utility horse and is able to work on the farm, pull the family cart and be used as a riding horse or hunter. In World War I they were used by the cavalry for pulling the heavy artillery. Prior to the Great War the breed flourished but the numbers dropped dramatically as a result of deaths in the war and mechanisation on farms. The breed has teetered on the brink of extinction but in 1976 a group of enthusiastic breeders formed the Irish Draught Horse Society to help preserve this strong, docile breed.

The breed's sensible qualities make it a great foundation horse to cross with the Thoroughbred to produce show jumpers, eventers, hunters and riding horses. Its strength and docile nature have made it an ideal horse for police forces worldwide.

34

Jutland

Native to
Denmark

Now found
Worldwide

Size
15hh – 16.1hh

Description

Chestnut, bay, grey or roan.

Denmark's own breed of heavy horse. The Jutland was used by the Vikings and the Romans as war horses and in the Middle Ages knights used them for jousting. They were also used in agriculture as draught horses.

The modern-day Jutland was developed during the mid 19th century when the native Danish breeds were crossed with the Suffolk, Cleveland and Ardennes. The major step in the development of the Jutland was the 1862 import from Britain of Oppenheim, a Suffolk/Shire stallion. He is considered to be the foundation of the breed. The majority of modern Jutlands can be traced back to his sons, Hovding and Prins af Jylland.

In 1928 the Carlsberg Brewery began using the Jutland for pulling drays. These horses are still used for shows, competitions and putting on demonstrations whilst promoting both the brewery and this docile breed.

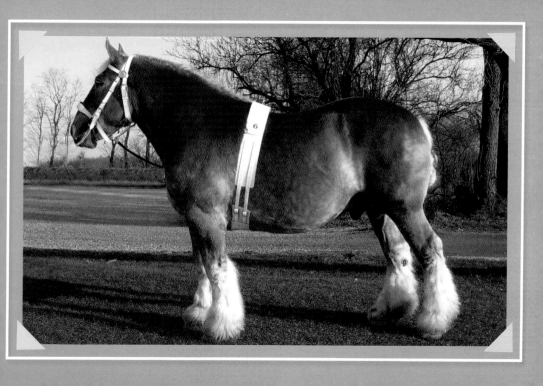

35

Lusitano

Native to
Portugal

Now found
Worldwide

Size
15.1hh – 15.3hh

Description

Any solid colour. Grey is the most common and other colours tend to go grey with age.

The Lusitano originated in the hilly and rough mountainous terrain of Portugal. These surroundings have produced a horse that is agile, courageous and hardy. The good looks of the elegant Lusitano are purely by chance as it has always been bred for ability rather than appearance.

The breed's exceptional ability has been known for over 5000 years and it was once used as a farm horse and a war horse. On the battlefield it was able to out-manoeuvre any opponent and had an amazing gift of second guessing its rider's thoughts whilst keeping him safe and carrying out the job in hand. In the 1600s the Spanish started selectively breeding the Lusitano for riding and parade work since its powerful presence and flashy gait made it a joy to watch.

Today, the Lusitano's talents can be seen in disciplines such as dressage, carriage driving and show jumping. Intelligent and courageous, athletic and level-headed. No, not me, the Lusitano.

36

Morgan

Native to
The USA

Now found
Throughout the British Isles
and on most continents

Size
14.1hh- 15.2hh

Description

Most common colours are bay, black and chestnut.

Every registered Morgan can be traced back to a single stallion born in 1789 called Figure but later renamed Justin Morgan after his owner, an impoverished school teacher who took the stallion in payment for a bad debt. Figure died in 1821 aged 32.

In the early years the Morgan earned a living hauling ploughs and logs but by the 1800s the natural elegance of the breed had promoted it to pulling the carriages of Boston blue-bloods and bankers. During this period harness racing reached its peak and Figure's great-grandson became the 'World's Fastest Trotting Stallion'.

Many Morgans still worked the land but because of their strength and reliability they were used by the Pony Express. They were later used by the military as cavalry horses in the American Civil War and a few years later a Morgan was the sole survivor at the Battle of the Little Big Horn.

Figure's descendants excel whether ridden or driven. They are strong, gentle and highly intelligent.

37

New Forest

Native to
The British Isles

Now found
In Europe, North America
and Australia

Size
12hh – 16.2hh

Description

New Forest colours are bay, brown, chestnut, grey, roan and black.

The New Forest pony has been around since at least the 11th century. King Canute's Forest Law of 1016 records wild horses and other animals in the New Forest. The ponies are now all privately owned but roam freely throughout the forest. The owners pay for a grazing right and each pony carries a brand with its owner's mark.

The ponies were originally used on smallholdings and as a draught animal, and have been known as a good children's pony since the reign of James I. Since its beginning there have been constant 'improvements' to the breed. The main introductions were the Welsh, Thoroughbred, Arab and Hackney. The private New Forest Society formed in 1884 became a public society in 1891. The breed stud book was closed in 1935 and only registered New Forest stallions are allowed to run with the forest mares.

The pony is intelligent, calm and agile so is ideal as a family pony or riding pony for the disabled. An exceptional all-rounder.

38

Percheron

Native to
The Perche area of
North West France

Now found
Worldwide

Size
Usually 16.2hh – 17.3hh

Description

Percherons are grey or black with a minimum of white.

At the Battle of Tours almost 1300 years ago the Moors were defeated and abandoned their horses. The abandoned Arabs were crossed with local Flemish stock and the result was the ancestors of the Percheron.

In the Middle Ages the Percheron was used as a battle horse carrying armour-laden knights. The invention of guns and gunpowder saw the Percheron retired from the battlefield and into a safer environment, hauling heavy stagecoaches around the French countryside. Once again redundancy loomed with the coming of the railway and the Percheron moved into agriculture as a draught horse. The traditional rocking horse is modelled on the Percheron.

Percherons are ideal for modern logging operations in difficult areas and do not require wide access roads or churn up the land. Cross a Percheron with a Thoroughbred and you have an excellent heavy hunter. Versatile, elegant and intelligent, what a combination!

39

Shetland

Native to
The Shetland Isles

Now found
On most continents

Size
10.2hh maximum in Britain

Description

A Shetland can be almost any colour: black; chestnut; bay; brown; grey; palomino; dun; roan; skewbald and piebald.

Shetland ponies have inhabited the Shetland Isles for over 2000 years. Archaeological evidence indicates that the pony was a domesticated breed in the Bronze Age. It is believed the breed's ancestors were Scandinavian ponies which arrived on Shetland at the end of the last Ice Age. Interbreeding between these new arrivals and the Norse and Celtic ponies created a breed able to survive on scarce food supplies and in extreme weather conditions. They have a double winter coat, long manes and thick tails that help them survive this harsh environment.

The Mines Act of 1847 forbade women and children under the age of 10 from working in the mines. The Shetland became pit ponies, taking over pulling and pushing heavy tubs filled with coal and ore and being greatly loved by their handlers. Long-lived, good-tempered and extremely intelligent, the Shetland is generally gentle but can be stubborn if handled unsympathetically. An ideal children's pony.

40

Shire

Native to
The British Isles

Now found
Worldwide

Size
16hh – 18hh

Protection category

Description

Black, brown, grey or bay.

The Shire is the English Great Horse. The largest and tallest of the modern heavy horses. Their ancestors came to the British Isles with William the Conqueror in 1066. The Great Horse of medieval times was developed to be large and strong enough to carry knights in battle armour.

During the 1700s Friesian and Flanders horses were imported to work on draining the Fens, these were crossed with the Great Horse and the Shire was born. The horses pulled carriages and carts around Britain on rutted, muddy 'roads' little better than cart tracks. The Shire was, for many years, the transport system of the British Isles. The English Cart Horse Society was formed in 1876 and in 1884 it became the Shire Horse Society.

During both World Wars the Shire reverted to a battle horse and hauled heavy artillery but by 1950 mechanisation had pushed it to the point of extinction. A dedicated group of breeders started to use them for local delivery work and the Shire now provides natural horse power.

41

Suffolk

Native to
Suffolk in England

Now found
Throughout the British Isles,
America, Canada, Australia
and New Zealand

Size
16.1hh – 17.1hh

Protection category

Description

Suffolks are chesnut (traditionally no 't' after the 's') in seven shades: bright; red; golden; yellow; light; dark and dull.

The Suffolk has the longest unbroken written pedigree record of any breed. It goes back to 1768 and a stallion called Crisp's Horse of Ufford. The Suffolk dates back to the 1500s but all today's animals can be traced back to this stallion.

Many hundreds of Suffolks once worked the farms of East Anglia but it was not until the 1930s that the Suffolk moved out of its remote and isolated home area. Several new studs were started outside Suffolk but unfortunately this coincided with the opening shots of World War II. There was a need to dramatically increase food production and that could only be achieved by, you guessed it, mechanisation. Larger farms were selling up to 40 horses a day but the only buyers were the slaughter houses. Sadly, matters deteriorated and during 1966 only 10 foals were born in the whole of the British Isles. Extinction was waiting in the wings. A group of new breeders came to the rescue and the breed has edged back from the brink but is still listed as critical.

42

Thoroughbred

Native to
England

Now found
Worldwide

Size
15.2hh – 17hh

Description

Bay, brown, chestnut, black or grey.

The Thoroughbred is a breed, although the term is also used (some would say misused) to describe any breed that is purebred. The Thoroughbred is possibly best known as a racehorse.

The Thoroughbred dates back to the 17th and 18th centuries and their ancestors can be traced back to three stallions - Byerley Turk, Darley Turk and Godolpin Arabian - who were imported to improve the local mares and established the modern Thoroughbred. In the early 20th century only British-bred horses could be registered in the General Stud Book, thereby eliminating all American Thoroughbreds. This ruling was repealed in 1949 and now horses are accepted if 9 previous generations have been registered in an accepted studbook.

Not all Thoroughbreds are born to race; some are hunters, sprinters and chasers as well as all-rounders which are capable of all of the above. The Thoroughbred is the greyhound of the horse world: sleek; elegant; smooth muscles; long legs; highly intelligent; sensitive and, would you believe, temperamental.

43

Welsh Pony

Native to
Wales

Now found
Worldwide

Size
13.2hh maximum

Protection category

Description

The Welsh pony is mainly black, brown, grey, bay, roan, cream or chestnut.

A truly ancient breed which wandered the hills and valleys of Wales long before the Romans set foot in Britain. They were influenced by Roman horses which arrived during the occupation and Arab stallions which returned with the Crusaders. The Welsh has been as it is today since the 15th century .

In 1548 Henry VIII issued instructions that all horses under 15 hands were to be destroyed, thereby creating a minimum standard size for horses. All horses would then be of a size suitable for war or battle should they be required. Fortunately, the Welsh ponies lived in remote, inaccessible places and were not culled by the long sword of the Royal decree. Their remote habitats also saved the lives of the Dartmoor and Exmoor ponies. When Elizabeth I came to the throne the law was reversed.

The Welsh pony can be used as a draught animal and competes in all forms of equestrianism. They are tough, steady, calm and loved by children and adults alike.

Kaimanawa

Native to
New Zealand

Size
10hh–13hh

The Kaimanawa can be any horse colour.

Horses were introduced into New Zealand in 1814 and in 1876 the first wild horses were to be seen in the mountainous regions of Kaimanawa. Over the years other local and imported breeds have escaped or been released into the area and their genes have added to the strength of the Kaimanawa Wild Horse.

In 1981 the Kaimanawa Wild Horse was given a protected status and numbers increased. Now this status has been removed as many as 1200 are being rounded up or culled to protect rare plants and grasses. The numbers left would not leave a viable breeding group.

Lac La Croix

Native to
Canada

Size
12.2hh – 14.2hh

The Lac La Croix is any single colour except white.

This very rare Canadian pony developed from cross breeding between Spanish horse and French heavy horses.

In 1977 the breed was close to extinction and the Ojibwa Native Americans rescued the 4 remaining mares. With the help of a few dedicated breeders and Rare Breeds Canada the numbers have increased to approximately 100.

The Lac La Croix Indian pony has nostril flaps, profusely haired ears and an extremely thick coat to keep out the Canadian winter. They are gentle, hardy, versatile and an important part of world history.

Sable Island

Native to
The Sable Islands, Canada

Size
Around 14hh

The Sable Island is any horse colour.

These horses were confiscated from the French Colonists during the Acadian Expulsions of 1755. A ship owner, paid to transport the Acadians to the American Colonies, took 60 horses which he put out to pasture on Sable Island.

Initially the horses worked as part of brave rescue teams that assisted boats that foundered on nearby rocks. The herd is now feral and numbers between 250 and 400 horses.

Visitors to Sable Island are restricted and the horses must not be disturbed in any way. One of the world's true wild horses.

RBST
Rare Breeds Survival Trust

The Watchlist covers sheep, cattle, pigs, goats, poultry, horses & ponies.

A breed whose numbers of registered breeding females are estimated by the Rare Breeds Survival Trust to be below the category 6 "Mainstream" threshold will be accepted into the appropriate Watchlist category. In this book I have highlighted the first five categories.

🐏 Critical

🐏 🐏 Endangered

🐏 🐏 🐏 Vulnerable

🐏 🐏 🐏 🐏 At Risk

🐏 🐏 🐏 🐏 🐏 Minority

Further information: www.rbst.org.uk

Horse Talk

Stallion	An adult male horse
Gelding	A castrated adult male horse
Mare	An adult female horse
Foal	A young horse under one year old.
Draught Horse	A horse used for drawing heavy loads such as a plough or a cart.
Gaits	A horse's paces
Warmblood	These horses are mainly sport-horses such as those used in polo, show jumping and dressage.
Coldblood	These horses are draught animals so are large and heavily muscled; built to work.

Colours

Piebald	Large irregular patches of black and white
Skewbald	Large irregular patches of brown and white
Roan	A dark coat with hairs of patches of white or grey
Bay	A brown coat with a black mane and tail
Dun	A golden coat with a black mane and tail and black dorsal stripe
Palomino	A golden coat with white mane and tail
Flaxen	A flaxen mane and tail is pale cream or white. It almost always occurs with a chestnut coat
Chestnut	A ginger coat with mane and tail the same colour

Measuring Horses

Horses are measured at their withers which is the high point where the neck meets the body.

Horses are measured in hands and inches. A hand is 4 inches (originally measured across the breadth of the hand).

Horses are generally those over 14.2hh (hands high) and ponies are generally under 14.2hh. There are a few exceptions to this rule such as the Falabella. Ponies tend to be stockier, more resistant to bad weather or cold and stronger for their size than horses.